Tiny Life in the Air

By Christine Taylor-Butler

Consultants
Reading Adviser
Nanci Vargus, EdD
Assistant Professor of Literacy
University of Indianapolis
Indianapolis, Indiana

Subject Adviser
Howard A. Shuman, PhD
Department of Microbiology
Columbia University Medical Center
New York, New York

Children's Press®
A Division of Scholastic Inc.
New York   Toronto   London   Auckland   Sydney
Mexico City   New Delhi   Hong Kong
Danbury, Connecticut

Designer: Herman Adler Design
Photo Researcher: Caroline Anderson
The photo on the cover shows lily pollen.

Library of Congress Cataloging-in-Publication Data

Taylor-Butler, Christine.
  Tiny life in the air / by Christine Taylor-Butler; consultant, Nanci R. Vargus.
    p. cm. — (Rookie read-about science)
  Includes index.
  ISBN 0-516-25273-9 (lib. bdg.)   0-516-25476-6 (pbk.)
  1. Air—Microbiology—Juvenile literature. I. Vargus, Nanci Reginelli.
II. Title. III. Series.
  QR101.T39 2005
  579'.175—dc22   2005004630

CHILDREN'S PRESS, and ROOKIE READ-ABOUT®,
and associated logos are trademarks and/or registered trademarks
of Scholastic Library Publishing. SCHOLASTIC and associated logos
are trademarks and/or registered trademarks of Scholastic Inc.

1 2 3 4 5 6 7 8 9 10 R 14 13 12 11 10 09 08 07 06 05

Tiny living things float in the air around you. Can you see them?

No, you can't!
They are too small.

Scientists can see them
with microscopes.

6

Do you think dust is small?

These tiny living things
are smaller than dust!
They are so small that
they can live inside dust.

Sometimes the wind carries the dust across the ocean. The trip can take a week.

The dust finally lands. Now the tiny life lives on a new continent.

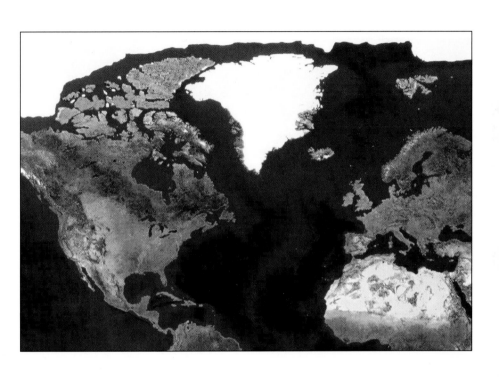

9

10

Some tiny life can live in places where others cannot. This place is Antarctica. It is very cold here.

Some tiny life forms have thick skin. The skin helps the tiny life live here.

Mold and fungus are kinds of tiny life.

Many molds and funguses can group together. Then you can see them.

13

14

This is a spore. Molds and funguses shoot spores into the air.

Spores are like seeds. New molds and funguses grow from the spores.

The spores travel through the air. The spores have all the food they need. They will be okay in the air until they find a home.

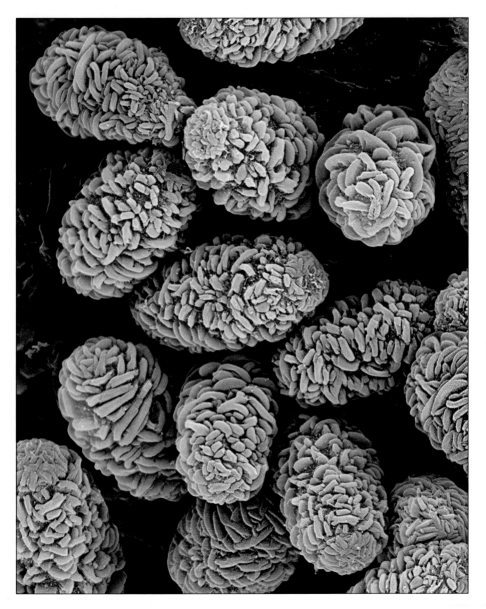

17

18

Spores look for wet places to land.

After they land, they begin to grow. They will turn into molds or funguses that you can see.

Bacteria (bak-TIHR-ee-uh) is a kind of tiny life. Some bacteria float in the air.

Bacteria can be many different shapes. What shapes do you see here?

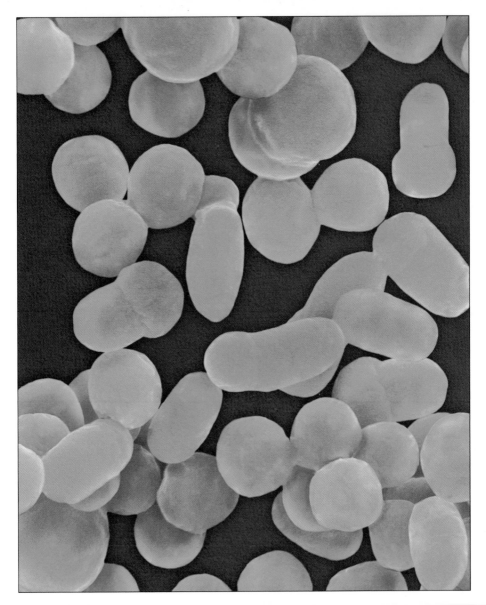

21

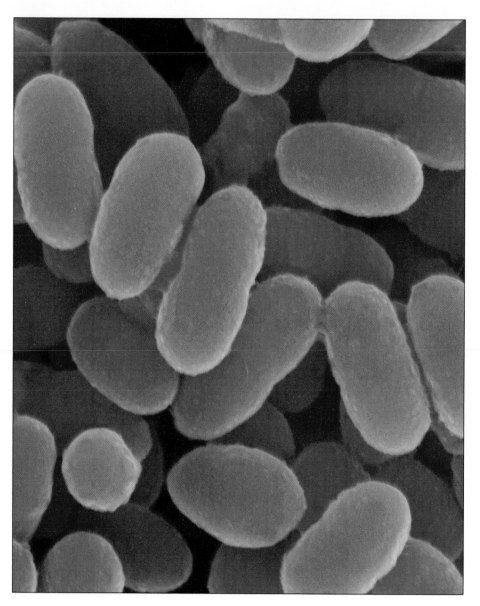

22

Some bacteria can make you sick if they get into your body. These bacteria are called germs.

A virus is another kind of tiny life that floats in the air.

A virus is smaller than bacteria. Viruses make people sick, too.

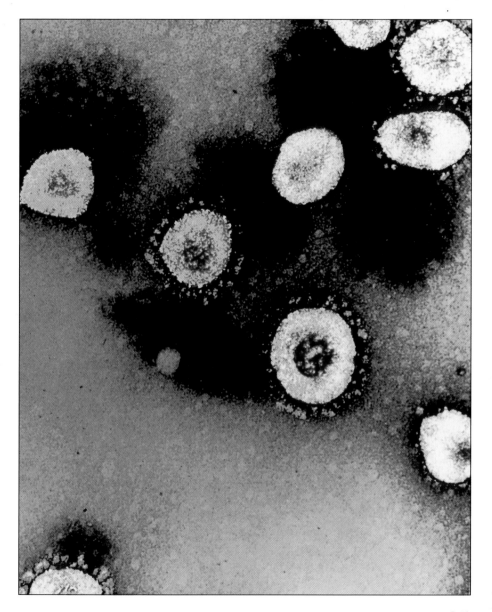

25

26

When you sneeze, you shoot bacteria and viruses into the air. Other people could get sick from the bacteria and viruses.

You should use a tissue when you sneeze.

Not all tiny life is bad. Many tiny living things are good. They fight the bad bacteria and viruses.

You can't see them, but tiny life forms are floating all around you!

Words You Know

Antarctica

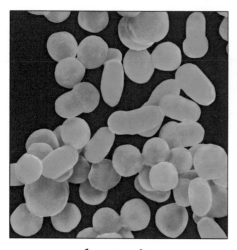

bacteria

funguses

microscope

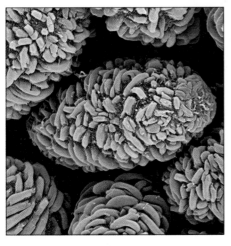

spores

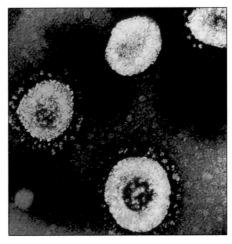

viruses

Index

About the Author

Christine Taylor-Butler is the author of nineteen books for children and adults. In addition to her fiction titles, she has written a nonfiction series about the planets. Formerly an engineering manager with Hallmark Cards, Ms. Taylor-Butler holds two degrees from the Massachusetts Institute of Technology. She now lives in Kansas City, Missouri, with her husband, Ken, two daughters, a pride of mischievous black cats, and two tanks of anxious but safely contained fish.

Photo Credits

Photographs © 2005: Corbis Images/Clouds Hill Imaging Ltd.: 13; Getty Images: 21, 30 bottom left (Dr. Dennis Kunkel/Visuals Unlimited), 10, 30 top (Maria Stenzel/National Geographic); Peter Arnold Inc.: 25, 31 bottom right (CDC), 6 (David Scharf); Photo Researchers, NY/David M. Phillips: cover; PictureQuest/Adrian Peacock: 5, 31 top; Superstock, Inc.: 26 (Image Source), 29 (Jon Smyth); Taxi/Getty Images/Felix Labhardt: 14, 30 bottom right; The Image Bank/Getty Images/Image Makers: 9; The Image Works: 3 (Esbin/Anderson), 18 (Topham); Visuals Unlimited/Dr. Dennis Kunkel: 17, 22, 31 bottom left.